Published By Adam Gilbin

@ Marc Ellis

Weight Loss : How to Use Apple Health,smoothie

Book for Weight Loss , Weight Loss Smoothie

Recipes

All Right RESERVED

ISBN 978-87-94477-68-0

TABLE OP CONTENTS

Oatmeal Porridge 1

Easy Weight Loss Daal 3

Easy Weight Loss Vegetable Soup 5

Vegetable Upma 6

Soya Chunks Vegetable Pulao 9

Cucumber Raita 12

Warm Lemon H2y Water... 14

Meth Seeds Soaked Water 15

Warm Water With H2y And Cinnamon 16

Berry Bliss Delight.. 17

Tropical Turmeric Twist 19

Citrus Zing Refresher 21

Chocolate Banana Protein Power.................................... 23

Blueberry Banana Oat Muffins 25

Berries With Yoghurt Sheet Pan Pancakes 27

Burrito Bowl For Breakfast With Spiced Butternut Squash 31

Smoothie With Banana, Avocado, And Greens 34

Green Smoothies With Milk 36

Smoothie With Spinach And Yoghurt 38

Low-Fat Frittata Flat Belly Diet Recipe 39

Low-Calorie Salad To Shrink The Belly And Lose Weight 42

Quinoa And Vegetable Stir Fry 44

Vegetable Omelet With Eggs, Spinach, Tomatoes, And Feta Cheese 46

Whole Grain Bread 48

Baked Chicken Breast With Roasted Vegetables And Couscous 51

Egg White Omelet With Veggies: 54

Turkey Lettuce Wraps 56

Grilled Salmon With Asparagus 57

Green Machine Juice 58

Ginger Citrus Blast 59

Broccoli Blast 60

Healthy Spring Vegetable Frittata 62

Red And Green Breakfast Salad 64

Italian Hash With Eggs 67

Meatball & Tomato Soup 69

Bacon & Mushroom Pasta 71

Warm Chorizo & Chickpea Salad 73

Roast Spiced Duck With Plums 75

Lobster Breakfast Burritos 78

Quinoa Breakfast Bowl 80

Zero Belly Fruit Salad 81

Busting Smoothie Recipe 83

Detox Water For A Flat Belly 84

Low-Calorie Salad To Shrink The Belly And Lose Weight 85

Turkey Meat Loaf With Walnuts And Sage 87

Spicy Olive And Turkey Pita Sandwich 90

Roasted Potatoes With Blue Cheese-Walnut "Butter" .. 92

Banana Pancakes With Walnut Honey 94

Spinach And Paneer Curry 96

Sambhar 99

Moong Daal Soup 102

Pomegranate Blueberry Burst 104

Minty Mango Mojito 106

Avocado Bliss Booster 108

Cinnamon Apple Pie Delight 109

Tropical Green Tea Infusion 110

Healthy Biscotti Pumpkin 112

Handmade Potato Cakes 115

Steel-Cut Oats With Lemon Blueberries 117

Hazelnut And Pumpkin Flaugnarde Clafoutis 119

Smoothie With Tropical Green Blast 121

Smoothie Caramel Banana Green 122

Mango Spinach Green Smoothie 123

Spinach And Feta Omelet With Whole Grain Toast 124

Capers Salad With Fresh Mozzarella, Tomatoes, Basil Leaves, And Balsamic Glaze 126

Grilled Lamb Chops With Roasted Sweet Potatoes And Greek Salad 128

Hummus With Whole Grain Crackers And Carrot Sticks
.... 131

Oatmeal Porridge

Ingredients:

- A cup of skimmed milk,
- A tablespoon of h2y optional
- Half a cup of rolled oats,
- A tablespoon of mixed nuts

Directions:

1. Once you have all your Ingredients:preprepared, it's time to start cooking.
2. Start by adding the oats and milk to a saucepan, and heat it up on medium heat until it starts boiling.
3. Then, reduce heat to low and continue cooking for another five minutes, stirring occasionally.

4. Once the oats are cooked, add the h2y little by little, and keep stirring until it's fully absorbed.
5. Lastly, add the mixed nuts and stir everything.
6. And there you have it! Your delicious oatmeal porridge with skimmed milk weight loss easy recipe is ready to be served.

Easy Weight Loss Daal

Ingredients:

- Any Deal
- Medium Tomato
- Ginger
- Asafetida
- Coriander Leaves
- Jeer
- Red Chili Powder
- Turmeric Powder
- Chopped onion
- Oil

Directions:

1. Take 3 cups of dal, rinse them with clean water and soak for about 30 minutes.

2. Boil the lentils in 4 cups of water along with ginger and turmeric in a pressure cooker for about 3 whistles.
3. If the lentils are overcooked, strain the excess liquid and keep aside.
4. Take 1 tablespoon of oil in a pan and add asafoetida, jeera and sauté for a few seconds.
5. Now add the chopped onion and then crushed tomato into the pan. Add red chilli powder and fry until the tomato gets d2.
6. Lastly, add the boiled dal into the pan and allow it to cook for about 5 minutes.
7. Finally, add some fresh coriander leaves and remove it from the flame.
8. Your delicious and nutritious chana daal is ready to be served with chapatis.

Easy Weight Loss Vegetable Soup

Ingredients:

- 1 tomato
- Green peppers
- Salt
- Black pepper
- Coriander powder
- Cumin powder
- Garlic
- 1-2 carrots
- 1 potato
- 1 onion
- 2-3 cups of water

Directions:

1. Start by peeling and chopping the carrots, potatoes, onion, and tomato into small pieces. Slice the green peppers into small strips.
2. Get a pot and add the chopped vegetables.
3. Add 3 to 4 cups of water and bring the mixture to a boil.
4. Add spices such as salt, black pepper, coriander powder, cumin powder, and garlic to the boiling water. Leave the mixture to simmer for about 10 minutes.
5. Now, turn off the heat and let the soup rest for several minutes. Blend it with a blender or serve as it is.
6. And, that's it! Your delicious, Indian-style mixed vegetable soup is ready.

Vegetable Upma

Ingredients:

- 1 cup mixed vegetables like bell peppers, carrots, beans, peas, etc
- 2 green chilies
- 2 tablespoons oil
- 1/2 teaspoon mustard seeds
- 1/2 teaspoon cumin seeds
- 1 cup semolina suji
- 1 chopped onion
- 2 chopped tomatoes
- 1/2 teaspoon turmeric powder

Directions:

1. First of all, heat 2 tablespoons oil in a pan and add mustard and cumin seeds.
2. When the seeds start to crackle, add the onion and sauté it for a few minutes.
3. Now add the tomatoes and sauté for about a minute.

4. Next, add the mixed vegetables and sauté for a few minutes.
5. Now add the green chillies and sauté for a minute.
6. Now add the semolina and sauté for a few minutes, stirring continuously.
7. Add the turmeric powder and season with salt and sugar as per your taste.
8. Add 4 cups of water and stir continuously till the semolina is cooked.
9. And your delicious Vegetable Upma is ready. You can garnish the upma with freshly chopped coriander leaves.

Soya Chunks Vegetable Pulao

Ingredients:

- Black pepper 1 teaspoon
- Cinnamon stick 1 - 2 sticks
- Red chilli powder 1 teaspoon
- Cashews 1/4 cup
- Salt to taste
- Oil 2 tablespoons
- Basmati Rice 1 cup
- Vegetables 1 cup - bell pepper, onion, carrots, peas, coriander
- Soya chunks 1 cup
- Garlic cloves 2 - 3 cloves
- Jeera Cumin 1/2 teaspoon
- Cardamom 1 - 2 pods

- Cloves 3 - 4 pods
- Ghee 1 tablespoon

Directions:

1. First, let's prepare the vegetables and the soya chunks. Begin by washing the vegetables, and then cut them into small cubes.
2. Now add the soya chunks to a bowl, and mix it with half a teaspoon of salt and a spoon of oil. Set this aside.
3. Next, heat 2 tablespoons of oil in a deep pan over medium heat.
4. Once the oil is hot, add the cumin, cloves and cardamom, and let them crackle for about a minute.
5. Add the garlic cloves and stir for a few seconds. Now, add the chopped vegetables and salt and cook them for about 5 minutes. When the vegetables are cooked, add the soya chunks and mix.

6. Let's move on to the pulao. In the same pan, add ghee and give it a quick stir. Add the basmati rice and sauté it for a few minutes.
7. Now, add all the spices - chilli powder, pepper, cinnamon, and salt to taste. Mix everything well and allow it to cook for a few minutes more.
8. Finally, add 3 and a half 2 ½ cups of water and mix to combine.
9. Bring the mixture to a boil and then reduce the heat to low and cook for 15 minutes with the lid closed. Once the pulao is cooked, garnish it with the roasted cashews, and serve it hot.
10. Your delicious and healthy vegetable pulao with soya chunks is now ready. Enjoy!

Cucumber Raita

Ingredients:

- 1 teaspoon of cumin powder
- 2 tablespoons of fresh chopped cilantro
- 1 teaspoon of black pepper
- 1 large cucumber, peeled and diced or grated
- 1 cup Whisked yogurt
- 2 teaspoons of freshly squeezed lemon juice
- Salt to taste

Directions:

1. First, in a large bowl, mix the cucumber and yogurt.
2. Then, add in the freshly squeezed lemon juice, cumin powder, chopped cilantro, and black pepper.
3. Stir the mixture until all Ingredients:are well combined.

4. Finally, season the mixture with salt to taste.
5. Your Cucumber Raita is now ready to be served!

Warm Lemon H2y Water

Ingredients:

- 1 Glass of warm water.
- 2 Tablespoons of lemon juice.
- 1 Teaspoon of h2y

Directions:

1. In a glass of warm water, add 2 tablespoons of fresh lemon juice, and 1 teaspoon of h2y.
2. Mix it properly and have it every morning in an empty stomach.
3. This helps you to kick start your body and performs great for the whole day!
4. This combination helps you lose the extra fat and further maintain the metabolic rate in our body.

Meth Seeds Soaked Water

Ingredients:

- 1 Teaspoon of Methi seeds
- 1 Cup of water

Directions:

1. Start by taking a teaspoon of Methi seeds in a glass and pour some water over it.
2. Let it sit overnight. In the morning, strain the Methi seeds and the water is ready to drink.
3. Make sure the water is freshly made daily.

Warm Water With H2y And Cinnamon

Ingredients:

- 1 teaspoon of h2y, and
- 1 teaspoon of ground cinnamon powder
- 1 cup of lukewarm water,

Directions:

1. Start by pouring 2 cup of lukewarm water into a glass.
2. Then, add 1 teaspoon of h2y and 1 teaspoon of ground cinnamon powder to the water and mix well until the Ingredients:are fully combined.
3. You can also add a few drops of freshly squeezed lemon juice if you like.
4. Now your drink is ready.
5. All you need to do is drink it in the morning, after which you should not consume anything else for the next 45 minutes.

Berry Bliss Delight

Ingredients:

- 1/4 cup rolled oats
- 1 tablespoon flax seeds
- 1 tablespoon h2y
- 1 cup water or coconut water
- 1/2 cup mixed berries strawberries, blueberries, raspberries
- 1/2 cup plain Greek yogurt
- 1/2 cup kale leaves, stems removed
- Ice cubes optional

Directions:

1. Combine mixed berries, Greek yogurt, kale leaves, rolled oats, flaxseeds, and h2y in the blender.
2. Add water or coconut water to the mix.

3. Blend until smooth and creamy.
4. Add ice cubes if you like a cooler consistency and mix again.
5. Pour into a glass and experience the delightful Berry Bliss Delight!

Tropical Turmeric Twist

Ingredients:

- 1 teaspoon turmeric powder
- 1/2 teaspoon ginger, grated
- 1 tablespoon coconut flakes
- 1 cup coconut water
- 1/2 cup pineapple chunks
- 1/2 mango, peeled and chopped
- 1/2 banana
- Ice cubes optional

Directions:

1. Combine pineapple chunks, mango, banana, turmeric powder, shredded ginger, and coconut flakes in the blender.
2. Pour in coconut water for a tropical touch.

3. Blend until smooth, adding ice cubes if a cooler consistency is required.
4. Pour into a glass and take yourself to the tropics with the Tropical Turmeric Twist!

Citrus Zing Refresher

Ingredients:

- 1 tablespoon h2y
- 1 tablespoon chia seeds
- 1 cup water or orange juice
- Ice cubes optional
- 1 orange, peeled and segmented
- 1/2 grapefruit, peeled and sliced
- 1/2 cup carrots, chopped
- 1/2 cup plain yogurt

Directions:

1. Combine orange segments, grapefruit segments, diced carrots, yogurt, h2y, and chia seeds in the blender.
2. Add water or orange juice to the mix.

3. Blend until smooth, adding ice cubes as desired.
4. Pour into a glass and enjoy the Citrus Zing Refresher's rush of vitamin C and refreshing flavor!

Chocolate Banana Protein Power

Ingredients:

- 1 tbsp almond butter
- 1 cup unsweetened almond milk
- 1/2 teaspoon vanilla extract
- Ice cubes optional
- 1 banana frozen for a creamier texture
- 1 tablespoon cocoa powder
- 1 scoop of chocolate protein powder

Directions:

1. Place frozen banana, cocoa powder, chocolate protein powder, almond butter, almond milk, and vanilla extract in the blender.
2. Blend until smooth and creamy.
3. Add ice cubes and mix again for additional coolness.

4. Pour into a glass and enjoy the Chocolate Banana Protein Power.

Blueberry Banana Oat Muffins

Ingredients:

- 3/4 cup of almond milk without sugar
- 2 tsp vanilla
- Oats, 3 cups
- A smidgeon of baking powder
- Mashed 2 medium banana
- 2 egg
- 1/4 cup of brown sugar
- a single cup of blueberries

Directions:

1. Set aside a 12-cup muffin tin that has been sprayed with nonstick spray and preheated at 350 degrees Fahrenheit.

2. If you have an electric hand mixer, use it to combine the brown sugar and mashed banana. Add the vanilla and milk, and stir.
3. Next, mix in the baking powder and oats. Finally, fold in the blueberries very gently. The hitter will be a little bit runny.
4. After filling 12 muffin tins, bake for 18 to 20 minutes.

Berries With Yoghurt Sheet Pan Pancakes

Ingredients:

- 2-and-a-half unleavened general-purpose flour

- 1/4 cup whole wheat flour white

- 3 teaspoons of sugar, granulated

- 3 tsp baking powder

- 2 tsp baking soda

- 2 tsp kosher salt

- 2 and a half cups plain yoghurt Stonyfield Organic, 0%

- 4-quarters cup milk

- Water, six tablespoons

- 3 big eggs

- 3 tablespoons of melted, then gently cooled unsalted butter

- 3 tsp powdered vanilla extract
- Half a cup of mixed berries blueberries, raspberries, and blackberries, either fresh or frozen
- Fresh berries, powdered sugar, maple syrup, h2y, or yoghurt are optional toppings.

Directions:
1. Preheat the oven to 425 degrees Fahrenheit and move the rack to the middle position.
2. Cooking spray applied to the rim of an 18" x 13" sheet pan will help hold the parchment in place.
3. Cut a 16 × 20-inch piece of parchment paper to thoroughly cover the bottom. Place on the sheet pan, then mist the parchment and the sheet pan's sides with more oil.
4. Mix all of the dry Ingredients:flour to salt in a medium-sized bowl.

5. Mix the wet Ingredients:yoghurt to vanilla in a separate medium-sized bowl until well blended.
6. After adding the wet Ingredients:to the dry 2s in the bowl, stir until barely mixed. Avoid over-mixing or becoming concerned if lumps remain.
7. Add the berries and fold carefully.
8. Fill the baking sheet with the batter. Using a spatula, uniformly spread the batter. Then, hit the sheet pan on the counter a few times to settle the mixture.
9. Bake, flipping the pan halfway through, for 15 to 17 minutes.
10. Let the pancakes cool in the pan for five minutes. Then, slide a large cutting board over the top of the pan and turn the pancakes out onto the board. Cut into sixteen squares, then serve right away.

11. Reheat from frozen by heating for 45 seconds on a dish that is safe to use in the microwave, then flipping and cooking for an additional 45 seconds, or until thoroughly cooked.
12. Store: Allow it to cool fully, then place it in a zip-lock bag or airtight container in the refrigerator for four days.
13. To freeze: Allow it to cool fully before transferring it to a zip-lock bag or airtight container.
14. Pancakes may be reheated from the refrigerator by placing them on a microwave-safe dish and heating them for 40 seconds, rotating them halfway through.

Burrito Bowl For Breakfast With Spiced Butternut Squash

Ingredients:

- Ground pepper, fresh, to taste
- Sliced tomatoes in 2 cup
- 1/3 cup finely diced onion
- 1/4 cup of cilantro, shredded
- Half of a lime's juice
- Mist with olive oil
- Four big eggs.
- 4 ounces of diced Hass avocado
- 20 ounces of seeded and cubed butternut squash, measuring 1 inch in size
- 2 and a half tsp olive oil
- 3 tsp powdered garlic

- 2-half tsp cumin

- 2-half tsp smoked paprika

- 2-third tsp kosher salt

- 1/4 cup of shredded cheddar cheese with reduced fat

Directions:

1. Set oven temperature to 425°F. Grease a large nonstick baking sheet. Mix the squash, olive oil, cumin, smoked paprika, garlic powder, 1/2 teaspoon salt, and pepper in a medium-sized bowl. To coat, toss thoroughly. Evenly spread the squash onto a sheet pan, flipping it midway through. Roast for 20 to 25 minutes, or until golden and soft.

2. In the meanwhile, mix the tomatoes, onions, cilantro, and lime juice, and season with salt and pepper in a small dish. Put away.

3. Lightly coat a small pan with olive oil spray, add eggs, season with salt, cover, and cook over medium heat until the eggs are d2.
4. Layer 2/3 cup squash, 1/2 cup pico, 1-ounce avocado, 1 egg, and 1 tablespoon cheese in the bowls to construct them. Continue with the other bowls.

Smoothie With Banana, Avocado, And Greens

Ingredients:

- ½ avocados
- 1 lime, whole
- ½ cup fresh coconut flesh
- 1 cup baby spinach
- 1 cup Swiss chard
- 1 cup banana chunks, unripe
- ½ medium cucumbers
- 1 cup coconut water, unsweetened

Directions:

1. Thoroughly wash the spinach, Swiss chard, and cucumber under running water. Cut the cucumber into 1-inch cubes and chop the leaves.
2. Peel and cut bananas into 1-inch pieces.

3. Scoop out the avocado flesh. Remove the seed.
4. Peel and quarter the lime.
5. Puree the spinach, Swiss chard, and coconut water in a blender until smooth.
6. Add other Ingredients:and blend until smooth and blended well.
7. Strain into a large glass and serve.

Green Smoothies With Milk

Ingredients:

- ½ cup banana slices
- ½ lime fruit
- 3 cups kale leaves, chopped
- 1 medium-sized mango, entire
- 1 cup coconut milk, unsweetened

Directions:

1. Wash and prepare all of the ingredients. Remove the seed from the mango and cut it into 2-inch pieces. The lime fruit should be juiced.
2. Add the coconut milk to the mixer. Mix in the mango, banana, and lime juice. Last, add the kale leaves.
3. Mix all Ingredients:on high speed until the smoothie is creamy This will take about 30 seconds to process.

4. Pour into a glass and serve immediately.

Smoothie With Spinach And Yoghurt

Ingredients:

- 1 whole big orange
- 1/3 of a cup of strawberries
- 1/3 of a cup of plain yoghurt
- 2 cups spinach leaves, chopped
- ½ cup sliced bananas
- 1 cup of cubed ice

Directions:

1. Peel and cut oranges into pieces. If there are any seeds, remove them.
2. Put all items in a blender. Blend until smooth.
3. Pour into glasses and serve right away.

Low-Fat Frittata Flat Belly Diet Recipe

INGREDIENTS:

- 1/4cup cold water
- 1/2teaspoon dried tarragon or 1/2
- teaspoon fresh tarragon, finely chopped
- 1/2 teaspoon salt
- 2 ounces smoked salmon, thinly sliced, cut into 1/2-inch-wide pieces
- 2 teaspoons extra virgin olive oil
- 6 scallions, trimmed and chopped whites and 2-inch of green
- 6 large egg whites
- 4 large eggs
- 3/4 cup tapenade Black olive, MUFA

DIRECTIONS:

1. Preheat oven to 350°F.

2. Heat heavy 8" ovenproof sauté pan over medium heat 1 minute. Add oil and heat 20 seconds. Add scallions and sauté, stirring periodically with spatula, about 2 minutes or until soft.
3. Combine egg whites, eggs, water, tarragon, and salt in medium bowl. Whisk to blend. Season with freshly ground black pepper. Pour mixture into pan and lay salmon on top. Cook, stirring periodically, about 2 minutes or until partially set.
4. Transfer pan to oven and cook 12 to 14 minutes or until firm, golden, and puffed. Remove from oven. Use spatula to release frittata from pan. Gently slide onto warm serving platter, slice, and serve with 2 tablespoons of the tapenade.
5. Make it a Flat Belly Diet Meal.
6. For a well-balanced dish, thaw 1/2 cup of frozen dark sweet cherries 45 calories and

combine with 1 cup of fat-free plain Greek-style yogurt 112 calories. Top with 1/4 cup of toasted whole oats 75 calories.

Low-Calorie Salad To Shrink The Belly And Lose Weight

INGREDIENTS:

- 2 tablespoons chopped red onion 20 g
- 2 tablespoons chopped parsley 20 g
- ¼ cup of feta cheese 37 g
- 2 tablespoons of olive oil 32 g
- 1 tablespoon of red wine vinegar 10 ml
- ½ cups of cherry tomatoes 225 g
- a cucumber
- 1 ripe avocado
- Salt and pepper to taste

Directions:

1. Wash the cherry tomatoes, cut them in half and add them in a bowl.

2. Peel the cucumber, remove the seeds and dice it finely.
3. Remove the flesh of a ripe avocado and chop it in order to combine it with the ingredients already in the bowl.
4. Then, add the onion and chopped parsley, making sure they mix well with the other vegetables.
5. Add the feta cheese cut into cubes and stir carefully.
6. On the side, prepare a dressing with olive oil, red wine vinegar, salt and pepper.
7. Mix everything well and, after checking the flavor, pour it over the l0w-calorie salad.
8. Keep stirring gently so that delicate vegetables do not break.
9. Serve it and enjoy it.

Quinoa And Vegetable Stir Fry

Ingredients:

- 2 cloves garlic
- 1 red bell pepper
- 1 zucchini
- 1 tablespoon soy sauce
- 1 tablespoon honey
- 1 cup quinoa
- 2 cups water
- 1 tablespoon olive oil
- 1 small onion
- Salt and pepper to taste

Directions:

1. Rinse the quinoa and place it in a pot with 2 cups of water. Bring to a boil, then reduce heat to low and simmer for 15-20 minutes or

until the water is absorbed and the quinoa is cooked.
2. While the quinoa is cooking, heat the olive oil in a large skillet over medium-high heat.
3. Add the onion and garlic and cook for 2-3 minutes until the onion is translucent.
4. Add the bell pepper and zucchini and cook for an additional 5-7 minutes or until the vegetables are tender.
5. In a small bowl, whisk together the soy sauce and h2y.
6. Add the cooked quinoa and soy sauce mixture to the skillet with the vegetables and stir to combine.
7. Season with salt and pepper to taste.

Vegetable Omelet With Eggs, Spinach, Tomatoes, And Feta Cheese

Ingredients:

- 1/2 cup cherry tomatoes, halved
- 1/4 cup crumbled feta cheese
- 1 tbspn olive oil
- 4 large eggs
- 1 cup fresh spinach, chopped
- Salt and pepper to taste

Directions:

1. Beat the eggs thoroughly in a bowl. Add pepper and salt to taste.
2. In a nonstick skillet over medium heat, warm the olive oil.
3. Add the cherry tomatoes and chopped spinach to the skillet and cook for 2 to 3

minutes, or until the tomatoes are tender and the spinach has wilted.
4. Pour the beaten eggs on top of the skillet's vegetables.
5. Let the eggs cook without touching them for a few minutes, or until the edges begin to firm.
6. Use a spatula to gently lift the omelet's edges and tilt the pan to let any raw egg run to the edges.
7. Evenly cover the omelet with the crumbled feta cheese.
8. Cook the omelet for a further 2 to 3 minutes, or until the eggs are d2 and the cheese has melted.
9. To create a half-moon shape, use a spatula to fold 2 half of the omelet over the other.
10. Gently move the omelet to a serving dish. Right away serve the vegetable omelet

Whole Grain Bread

Ingredients:

- 1 can 14 ounces diced tomatoes
- 4 cups vegetable broth
- 1 bay leaf
- 1 teaspn dried oregano
- 1 teaspn dried thyme Salt and pepper to taste
- 2 tblspns olive oil
- Fresh parsley, chopped garnish
- 1 cup dried green lentils
- 1 onion, chopped
- 2 carrots, chopped
- 2 celery stalks, chopped
- 3 cloves garlic, minced
- 4 slices of whole grain bread

Directions:

1. After giving the lentils a cold water rinse, set them aside.
2. Heat the olive oil in a big pot over a medium heat.
3. Add the minced garlic, chopped celery, carrots, and onion to the pot. Vegetables should be sautéed for around 5 minutes until they start to soften.
4. Stir in the diced tomatoes and any fluids they may have.
5. Add the lentils that have been washed, the bay leaf, the dried oregano, and the dried thyme.
6. To taste, add salt and pepper.
7. Bring the soup to a boil before turning the heat down low and letting it simmer for about 40 minutes, or until the lentils are soft.
8. Toast the whole grain bread slices while the soup simmers.

9. After the lentils are cooked through, take the bay leaf out of the broth.
10. Arrange bowls with the Greek lentil soup and top each 2 with freshly chopped parsley.
11. Add a toasted whole grain piece of bread to each cup of soup.

Baked Chicken Breast With Roasted Vegetables And Couscous

Ingredients:

- 1 eggplant, cubed
- 2 tbspns olive oil
- 1 teaspn dried oregano
- 1 teaspn dried thyme
- Salt and pepper to taste
- 1 cup couscous
- 1 1/4 cups vegetable or chicken broth
- 4 b2less, skinless chicken breasts
- 2 bell peppers red, yellow, or a combination, sliced
- 2 zucchini, sliced
- Fresh parsley, chopped garnish

Directions:

1. Turn on the oven at 400 °F 200 °C.
2. Put the chicken breasts in an oven-safe dish. Sprinkle salt, pepper, dried thyme, dried oregano, and olive oil over top. To coat the chicken evenly, rub the seasonings on.
3. Arrange the cubed eggplant, cut bell peppers, and zucchini on a different baking sheet.
4. Add a drizzle of olive oil and some salt & pepper. Toss the vegetables in the oil and seasoning to evenly distribute them.
5. Put the dish containing the chicken and the vegetables in the preheated oven.
6. Bake the chicken for about 25 to 30 minutes, or until it is thoroughly cooked, and the vegetables are soft and slightly browned.
7. Make the couscous as directed on the package, but use vegetable or chicken broth for water while the chicken and vegetables are baking.

8. Use a fork to fluff the couscous before transferring it to a serving plate.
9. Take the roasted veggies and chicken out of the oven.
10. Include a serving of roasted veggies and couscous with each cooked chicken breast. Add freshly cut parsley as a garnish.

Egg White Omelet With Veggies:

Ingredients:

- 2 quarter cup diced mushrooms
- 2 quarter cup diced onions
- 2 quarter cup diced tomatoes
- 3 Egg Whites
- 2 quarter cup diced bell peppers
- Salt and pepper to taste

Directions:

1. In a small bowl, beat the egg whites until light and fluffy.
2. Heat a non-stick skillet over medium-high heat. Add the egg whites and scramble until cooked through.
3. Add the bell peppers, mushrooms, onions and tomatoes to the skillet and cook until softened, about 3 minutes.

4. Season with salt and pepper to taste.
5. Serve the omelet with a side of fresh fruit.

Turkey Lettuce Wraps

Ingredients:

- 3 tablespoons diced red onion
- 2 tablespoon diced celery
- 2 tablespoon diced carrots
- 3 tablespoons fresh parsley, chopped
- Half cup cooked turkey, diced
- 2 quarter cup low-fat Greek yogurt
- 3 leaves of lettuce, washed and separated

Directions:

1. In a medium bowl, combine the turkey, Greek yogurt, red onion, celery, carrots and parsley.
2. Divide the mixture into 3 and spoon onto the 3 lettuce leaves.
3. Roll up the lettuce leaves and enjoy.

Grilled Salmon With Asparagus

Ingredients:

- Half teaspoon olive oil
- Half teaspoon garlic powder
- Salt and pepper to taste
- 3 Four oz salmon fillets
- 2 cup steamed asparagus

Directions:

1. Preheat the grill to medium-high heat.
2. Rub the salmon fillets with olive oil, garlic powder, salt and pepper.
3. Place the salmon on the grill and cook for 4 minutes on each side, or until cooked through.
4. Serve the salmon with the steamed asparagus..

Green Machine Juice

Ingredients:

- 100g of cucumber
- 150g of apple
- 1/2 lemon juiced
- 100ml of water
- 100g of kale
- 100g of spinach
- 50g of celery

Directions:

1. Wash and chop all the Ingredients:into tiny pieces.
2. Extract the juice by placing all the Ingredients: into a juicer.
3. Juice until smooth and well-combined.
4. Serve the juice right away by pouring it into a glass.

Ginger Citrus Blast

Ingredients:

- 1 teaspoon of turmeric powder
- 1/4 teaspoon of black pepper
- 240 ml of water
- 100g of fresh ginger root
- 300g of oranges
- 1 lemon juiced

Directions:

1. Peel and chop the fresh ginger root into small pieces.
2. Squeeze the juice of 2 lemon and chop the oranges into pieces.
3. Place all the comp2ntes in a juicer.
4. Add the water and juice until smooth.
5. If preferred, garnish the juice with an orange slice or a sprig of fresh mint before serving.

Broccoli Blast

Ingredients:

- 10g slice of ginger
- 240ml of water
- Ice cubes optional
- 200g of broccoli
- 100g of green apple
- 30g of juiced lemon

Directions:

1. The broccoli and apple should be cleaned and cut into tiny pieces.
2. Ginger should be skinned and cut into tiny pieces.
3. Juice the lemon, then put the juice aside.
4. To a juicer, add the chopped broccoli, apple, and ginger. Process until smooth.

5. The combination should now be poured into a glass along with some water and lemon juice.
6. If ice is preferred, serve.

Healthy Spring Vegetable Frittata

Ingredients:

- Nonstick cooking spray
- 2 cups fresh asparagus cut into 1-inch pieces
- ½ cup chopped leek
- ½ cup chopped red bell pepper
- 4 cups fresh spinach
- 1 Tbsp olive oil
- 8 eggs
- ½ cup crumbled feta cheese
- 1 tsp snipped fresh dillweed
- ½ tsp snipped fresh thyme
- Salt and black pepper to taste

Directions:

1. In a large bowl, beat eggs. Add ¼ cup of the cheese, the dillweed, and thyme; whisk to combine. Set aside.
2. Coat a large nonstick skillet with cooking spray and heat over medium heat. Add asparagus, leek, and pepper. Cook for 4 minutes, stirring occasionally. Add spinach and cook until spinach is wilted, tossing with tongs. Add oil to skillet; toss to coat. Spread vegetables
3. evenly. Pour eggs over vegetables; do not stir. Cook over medium heat.
4. As mixture sets, run a spatula around the edge of the skillet, lifting egg mixture so uncooked portion flows underneath. Continue cooking and lifting egg mixture for about 10 minutes, until it is nearly set.
5. Sprinkle with remaining ¼ cup cheese.
6. Remove skillet from heat. Let stand, covered, for 3 to 4 minutes, or until top is set. Season with salt and pepper.

Red And Green Breakfast Salad

Ingredients:

- 2 slices whole-wheat bread, cubed
- 3 cups chopped stemmed kale
- 3 cups baby spinach
- 1 ½ cups cooked quinoa, chilled
- 4 cups water
- 1 Tbsp vinegar
- 8 eggs
- 1 lb asparagus, trimmed and cut into 2-inch pieces
- 1 lb cherry or grape tomatoes
- 6 cloves garlic, quartered
- 1 Tbsp plus 2 tsp extra-virgin olive oil
- 1 Tbsp red wine vinegar optional

- Salt and black pepper to taste

Directions:
1. Preheat oven to 425°F. Place asparagus, tomatoes, and garlic in a single layer on a 15 x 10 x 1-inch baking pan. Drizzle with 2 tsp oil.
2. Roast for 10 to 12 minutes, or until asparagus is tender. Place bread cubes on a rimmed baking sheet and bake for 5 minutes or until crisp and browned.
3. Portion kale and spinach into four serving bowls. Top with quinoa, roasted vegetables, and croutons.
4. Meanwhile, add the water and vinegar to a large skillet. Bring vinegar mixture to boiling; reduce heat to simmering. Break an egg into a cup and slip egg into the simmering water. Repeat with three
5. more eggs. Simmer eggs for 3 to 5 minutes, or until whites are

6. completely set and yolks begin to thicken but are not hard. Remove from water with a slotted spoon. Repeat with remaining four eggs.
7. Serve atop salad.
8. Drizzle with 1 Tbsp oil and the red wine vinegar, if desired. Season with salt and pepper.

Italian Hash With Eggs

Ingredients:

- 8 oz precooked Italian-style chicken sausage, quartered lengthwise
- and cut into ¼-inch slices
- 2 cups thinly sliced kale
- ¼ cup grated Asiago cheese
- Nonstick cooking spray
- 4 eggs
- 2 Tbsp olive oil
- 1 lb small red potatoes, cut into thin slices
- 1 ½ cups sliced cremini mushrooms
- ½ cup chopped fresh banana peppers
- ½ cup chopped onions
- 1 tsp Italian seasoning

- Salt and black pepper to taste

Directions:

1. In a large skillet, heat oil over medium heat. Add potatoes; cover and cook for 10 minutes, stirring once, until potatoes are nearly tender.
2. Add mushrooms, banana peppers, onion, and Italian seasoning; cook 3 minutes. Add sausage and kale; cook for 3 to 5 minutes, or until kale has wilted and all vegetables are tender. Sprinkle with cheese.
3. Meanwhile, spray a nonstick skillet with cooking spray. Heat over medium heat. Break eggs into skillet. Reduce heat to low; cook eggs for 3 to 4 minutes, or until whites are completely set and yolks start to thicken.
4. Serve fried eggs over hash. Season with salt and pepper.

Meatball & Tomato Soup

Ingredients:

- ½ tsp chilli flakes
- 2 x 400g cans chopped tomatoes
- 100g giant couscous
- 500ml hot vegetable stock
- 12 pork meatballs
- 150g baby spinach
- ½ small bunch of basil
- 1½ tbsp rapeseed oil
- 1 onion, finely chopped
- 2 red peppers, deseeded and sliced
- 1 garlic clove, crushed
- Grated parmesan, to serve optional

Directions:

1. Heat the oil in a saucepan. Fry the onion and peppers for 7 mins, then stir through the garlic and chilli flakes and cook for 1 min.
2. Add the tomatoes, giant couscous and veg stock and bring to a simmer.
3. Season to taste, then add the meatballs and spinach. Simmer for 5-7 mins or until cooked through. Ladle into bowls and top with the basil and some parmesan, if you like.

Bacon & Mushroom Pasta

Ingredients:

- 8 rashers streaky bacon
- 4 tbsp pesto fresh from the chiller cabinet if possible
- 200ml carton 50% fat crème fraîche
- 400g penne or other tube shape pasta
- 250g pack chestnut or button mushrooms, wiped clean
- Handful basil leaves

Directions:

1. Cook the pasta in boiling water in a large non-stick saucepan according to pack instructions.
2. Meanwhile, slice the mushrooms and snip the bacon into bite-size pieces with scissors or a sharp knife.

3. Reserve a few drops of the cooking water in a cup or bowl, then drain the pasta and set aside.
4. Fry the bacon and mushrooms in the same pan until golden, about 5 mins. Keep the heat high so the mushrooms fry in the bacon fat, rather than sweat.
5. Tip the pasta and reserved water back into the pan and stir over the heat for 1 min.
6. Take the pan off the heat, spoon in the pesto and crème fraîche and most of the basil and stir to combine. Sprinkle with the remaining basil to serve.

Warm Chorizo & Chickpea Salad

Ingredients:

- 2 red peppers, deseeded and cut into strips
- 400g can chickpeas, drained and rinsed
- 12 semi-dried tomatoes
- 1 tbsp red wine vinegar
- 280g pack cooking chorizo, sliced
- 1 large red onion, finely sliced
- 100g bag rocket, to serve

Directions:

1. In a large frying pan, dry-fry the chorizo until golden for about 10 mins, then use a slotted spoon to scoop it from the pan and set aside.
2. Add the onion and peppers to the pan and soften in the chorizo fat for 10 mins. Stir in the chickpeas and tomatoes, warming through.

3. Pour in the red wine vinegar and season.

   Serve in bowls with handfuls of rocket on top.

Roast Spiced Duck With Plums

Ingredients:

- 2 ½kg whole duck
- 1 tsp olive oil
- 6 plums, halved and st2d
- 3 bay leaves
- 75ml red wine vinegar
- 1 star anise
- 2 tbsp coriander seeds
- 4 tbsp muscovite sugar
- 300ml chicken stock

Directions:

1. Heat oven to 160C/140C fan/gas 4. Toast the star anise and coriander seeds in a dry pan until aromatic.

2. Tip the toasted spices into a spice grinder with 2 tsp sea salt and grind into a fine powder or crush using a pestle and mortar.
3. Put the spice salt in a bowl, add the sugar, mix well and set aside.
4. Lightly score the skin of the duck in a criss-cross pattern and heat the oil in a large casserole.
5. Using a pair of tongs to turn it, brown the duck well on all sides, pour off the excess fat, then sit the duck breast-side up and season all over with the sugar and spice mix.
6. Pack the plums around the outside, then scatter over the bay and pour over the vinegar and stock.
7. Roast in the oven for 2 hrs or until the duck is golden and the plums have broken down.
8. Turn the oven right up for 10 more mins to crisp up the skin.

9. Take the duck out of the pan to rest for 10 mins and spoon the excess fat off the plums. Carve the duck and serve with a good spoonful of plums.

Lobster Breakfast Burritos

Ingredients:

- 4 oz. of cooked lobster meat, chopped rough
- 1 pinch of cayenne pepper
- 1 tbsp. extra-virgin olive oil
- 4 free-range eggs
- ½ tsp. of fresh tarragon, chopped or dry
- Salt and ground black pepper to taste
- 3 home-made burritos see recipe

Directions:

1. Beat the eggs and fresh tarragon in a bowl. Set this aside.
2. Sprinkle the chopped lobster with the cayenne pepper.
3. Heat the olive oil in a skillet over medium-low heat. Add the chopped lobster, stirring, until warmed through.

4. Stir in the egg/tarragon mixture; increase the heat to medium and then scramble the eggs, stirring constantly, until done.
5. Spoon the scramble onto 3 warmed burritos, roll and serve with some home-made salsa.

Quinoa Breakfast Bowl

Ingredients:

- ½ cup of almond or coconut milk
- ½ cup of water
- ½ cup of rinsed quinoa

Directions:

1. Combine the quinoa, almond milk and water in a large saucepan and bring the mix to a boil then reduce the heat to a low simmer, continue stirring until most of the liquid has been absorbed by the quinoa.
2. Transfer the quinoa to a bowl and enjoy with sliced fruit and a little more almond milk.

Zero Belly Fruit Salad

Ingredients:

- 1 cup of pineapple, peeled, chopped
- 1 cup of orange juice
- 3 tbsp. chopped walnuts
- 1 cup of Greek yogurt
- 2 small bananas, peeled, chopped
- 2 cups of fresh mixed berries
- 1 red apple, seeded, cored, chopped
- 1 cup of red grapes
- 1 ripe peach, pitted, chopped

Directions:

1. Pour all prepared fruits into a large bowl with orange juice, mix up.
2. Spoon equal portions into 2 breakfast bowls
3. Drizzle Greek yogurt over the top

4. Sprinkle chopped walnuts to finish. Enjoy!

Busting Smoothie Recipe

INGREDIENTS:

- 2 tbsp Greek yoghurt
- 1 tbsp chia seeds
- 200 ml filtered water
- 2 tbsp Healthy Mummy Smoothie mix
- ½ red grapefruit peeled
- ½ cup mixed frozen berries

DIRECTIONS:

1. Blend all ingredients together in blender for 1-2 minutes. Enjoy!

Detox Water For A Flat Belly

Ingredients:

- 1 cucumber, sliced
- 1 lemon, sliced
- 6 c filtered water
- 1 tbsp. ginger, grated
- 1/3 c mint leaves

Directions:

1. Mix all of the Ingredients:together in a pitcher and store it in the fridge overnight, so that the flavors can infuse.
2. Drink it all the next day. It will help flush fat from your body.

Low-Calorie Salad To Shrink The Belly And Lose Weight

INGREDIENTS:

- tablespoons chopped parsley 20 g
- ¼ cup of feta cheese 37 g
- 2 tablespoons of olive oil 32 g
- 1 tablespoon of red wine vinegar 10 ml
- Salt and pepper to taste
- ½ cups of cherry tomatoes 225 g
- a cucumber
- 1 ripe avocado
- tablespoons chopped red onion 20 g

Directions:

1. Wash the cherry tomatoes, cut them in half and add them in a bowl.

2. Peel the cucumber, remove the seeds and dice it finely.
3. Remove the flesh of a ripe avocado and chop it in order to combine it with the ingredients already in the bowl.
4. Then, add the onion and chopped parsley, making sure they mix well with the other vegetables.
5. Add the feta cheese cut into cubes and stir carefully.
6. On the side, prepare a dressing with olive oil, red wine vinegar, salt and pepper.
7. Mix everything well and, after checking the flavor, pour it over the l0w-calorie salad.
8. Keep stirring gently so that delicate vegetables do not break.
9. Serve it and enjoy it.

Turkey Meat Loaf With Walnuts And Sage

INGREDIENTS:

- 2 slices whole wheat bread

- 1/4 cup fat-free milk

- 2 egg whites, lightly beaten

- 1 pound extra-lean ground turkey breast 99% fat-free

- 1/4 cup chopped fresh flat-leaf parsley

- 1/4 cup grated Parmesan cheese

- 1 tsp dried sage

- 2 tsp olive oil

- 1 large carrot, grated

- 4 scallions, thinly sliced

- 1 clove garlic, minced

- 1/2 cup walnuts MUFA

- 1/2 tsp salt
- 1/2 tsp freshly ground black pepper

Directions:

1. PREHEAT the oven to 350°F. Line a rimmed baking sheet with foil and coat the foil with olive oil spray.
2. HEAT the oil in a small nonstick skillet over medium heat. Add the carrot, scallions, and garlic and cook, stirring often, for about 3 minutes or until tender. Remove from the heat.
3. MEANWHILE, chop the walnuts in a food processor fitted with a metal blade. Break up the bread and add to the walnuts. Pulse until both are ground to fine crumbs.
4. Transfer to a large bowl. With a fork, stir in the milk and egg whites.
5. Add the turkey, parsley, cheese, sage, salt, pepper, and sautéed mixture. Mix gently just until blended.

6. SHAPE into a free-form loaf about 7" long and 4 1/2" wide on the prepared baking sheet. Bake for 50 to 60 minutes or until a thermometer inserted in the thickest portion registers 165°F. Let stand a few minutes before slicing.

Spicy Olive And Turkey Pita Sandwich

Ingredients:

- 1/8 tsp red-pepper flakes
- 1 whole wheat 6" diameter pita, halved crosswise
- 4 ounces deli-sliced lower-sodium turkey breast
- 1/2 cup mixed greens
- 10 pitted green pimiento-stuffed olives, chopped
- 10 pitted black olives, chopped
- 1 tsp balsamic vinegar
- 1 tsp extra virgin olive oil

Directions:

1. Combine the green and black olives, vinegar, oil, and red-pepper flakes in a small bowl.

2. Fill each pita half with 2 ounces turkey breast, 1/4 cup greens, and half of the olive mixture.

Roasted Potatoes With Blue Cheese-Walnut "Butter"

INGREDIENTS:

- 1/8 tsp salt

- 1/2 cup coarsely chopped walnuts

- 2 ounces crumbled blue cheese

- 2 scallions, thinly sliced

- 1 pound thin-skinned baby potatoes, halved

- 1½ tsp olive oil

- 1/4 tsp freshly ground black pepper

Directions:

1. Preheat the oven to 425°f. Coat a 9" baking dish with cooking spray or line with parchment paper. Place the potatoes in the prepared dish and toss with the oil, pepper, and salt. Turn cut side down in the pan. Roast

for 30 to 35 minutes or until very tender and lightly golden on the underside.

2. Meanwhile, put the walnuts in a small baking pan or skillet and place in the oven to toast for 6 to 8 minutes. Tip into a bowl and let cool. Add the blue cheese and scallions and crumble with your fingers.

3. When the potatoes are d2, turn them over and sprinkle evenly with the walnut mixture. Bake for 5 minutes longer or until the cheese is melted.

Banana Pancakes With Walnut Honey

Ingredients:

Pancakes

- 1 Tbsp canola oil

- 1 tsp vanilla extract

- 1 large banana, halved lengthwise and cut thin slices

- 1/2 c fresh raspberries

- 1 and 1/3 c Easy Pancake Mix or store-bought, trans-fat free pancake mix

- 1/4 tsp ground cinnamon

- 1 c low-fat buttermilk

- 1/4 c water

- 1 egg

Walnut Honey

- 1/2 c walnuts, chopped

- 1/3 c honey
- 1 Tbsp water

Directions:

1. Combine the pancake mix and cinnamon in a large bowl. Combine the buttermilk, water, egg, oil, and vanilla extract in a separate bowl.
2. Whisk into the pancake mix and stir until smooth. Fold in the banana. Set aside.
3. Combine the walnuts, honey, and water in a small bowl.
4. Coat a large nonstick skillet with cooking spray and set over medium heat.
5. Add the pancake batter in scant 1/4 cupfuls and cook, in batches, for about 2 minutes or until the pancakes have puffed and the undersides are lightly browned.
6. Turn the pancakes and cook for about 2 minutes longer or until lightly browned. Serve with the walnut honey and raspberries.

Spinach And Paneer Curry

Ingredients:

- 1 teaspoon of minced garlic
- 2 chopped green chilies
- 1 teaspoon of garam masala
- 1 teaspoon of cumin powder
- 1 teaspoon of coriander powder
- 1 teaspoon of red chili powder
- half teaspoon of turmeric powder
- 1 teaspoon of lemon juice
- 1 cup of chopped spinach
- 1 cup of diced paneer
- 1 tablespoon of vegetable oil
- 1 teaspoon of cumin seeds
- 1 teaspoon of minced ginger

- salt to taste

Directions:

1. Start by heating the oil over medium heat in a pan.
2. Add in the cumin seeds, and let them sizzle for a few seconds.
3. Then add in the minced ginger and garlic, and fry them until fragrant.
4. Now add in the chopped chilies, and fry for a few more seconds.
5. Then add the garam masala, cumin powder, coriander powder, red chili powder and turmeric powder.
6. Mix everything together and fry the spices until they become fragrant.
7. Now, add the spinach and paneer to the pan.
8. Mix everything together, and cook for five to seven minutes, or until the spices are absorbed by the vegetables.

9. Once the vegetables are cooked, add in the lemon juice and salt to taste. Simmer for 3 minutes, then turn off the heat.
10. And there you have it! Spinach and Paneer Curry - an easy and delicious Indian dish that's sure to satisfy your taste buds and help you reach your weight loss goals. Enjoy!

Sambhar

Ingredients:

- ½ teaspoon of turmeric powder
- 1 green chili, finely chopped
- 2 tomatoes, chopped
- ½ teaspoon of cumin powder
- 1 teaspoon of red chili powder
- 3 cups of water
- 1 teaspoon of tamarind paste
- 1 cup toor dal split pigeon peas
- 2 tablespoons of oil
- 1 onion, finely chopped
- 1 teaspoon of mustard seeds
- 1 teaspoon of cumin seeds
- 2 cloves of garlic, minced

- 1 teaspoon of coriander powder
- Salt to taste

Directions:
1. Take the toor dal in a pressure cooker and add 3 cups of water and some salt.
2. Cook the dal for about 5-6 whistles or until it is soft.
3. Once d2, take it off the heat and set aside.
4. In a pan, heat the oil and add the mustard seeds, cumin seeds and onion.
5. Saute until the onion turns golden brown.
6. Now add the garlic and saute for a few minutes.
7. Add the coriander powder, turmeric powder, cumin powder, red chili powder and green chili and mix it all together.
8. Add the tomatoes and saute until they are cooked.
9. Add the cooked dal and 4 cups of water and bring it to a boil.

10. Now add the tamarind paste and salt.
11. Simmer for about 15-20 minutes.
12. Finally, adjust the seasoning and samba is ready to be served.
13. Serve it with steamed rice and enjoy!

Moong Daal Soup

Ingredients:

- 2-3 cloves of garlic minced
- 2 tablespoons of freshly grated ginger
- 2 chopped tomatoes
- 1 teaspoon of turmeric
- 1 cup of split yellow moong daal
- 2 tablespoons of olive oil
- 1 teaspoon of cumin
- 1 cup of carrots peeled and chopped
- Salt to taste

Directions:

1. First, heat the oil in a pan over a low-medium heat.
2. Once hot, add in the cumin and let the aromas fill the air.

3. Then add in the garlic, ginger, and carrots and sauté until they become aromatic.
4. Next, add in the moong daal and mix until it is evenly coated in the oil.
5. Then, add in the tomatoes and turmeric and mix until it is all combined.
6. Finally, add 3 cups of water and salt to taste.
7. Bring the soup to a boil and then reduce the heat.
8. Simmer for about 15-20 minutes, stirring occasionally until the moong daal is cooked and the soup has thickened up.
9. Now the soup is ready! Serve it in individual bowls with a garnish of your choice and enjoy.

Pomegranate Blueberry Burst

Ingredients:

- 1 tablespoon h2y 1 tablespoon flax seeds
- 1 cup water or coconut water
- Ice cubes optional
- 1/2 cup blueberries
- 1/2 cup pomegranate seeds
- 1/2 cup Greek yogurt

Directions:

1. Combine blueberries, pomegranate seeds, Greek yogurt, h2y, and flaxseeds in the blender.
2. Pour in water or coconut water for a refreshing twist.
3. Blend until smooth, adding ice cubes if a cooler consistency is required.

4. Pour into a glass and experience the antioxidant-rich Pomegranate Blueberry Burst!

Minty Mango Mojito

Ingredients:

- 1/2 cup cucumber, peeled and sliced
- 1 tbsp chia seeds
- 1 cup coconut water
- 1 cup mango chunks fresh or frozen
- 1/2 lime, juiced
- 1 tablespoon fresh mint leaves
- Ice cubes optional

Directions:

1. Combine mango chunks, lime juice, fresh mint leaves, cucumber, and chia seeds in the blender.
2. Pour in coconut water for a tropical twist.
3. Blend until smooth, adding ice cubes as desired.

4. Pour into a glass and enjoy the Minty Mango MMojitos' refreshing and hydrating feelings!

Avocado Bliss Booster

Ingredients:

- 1 tablespoon hemp seeds
- 1 tablespoon h2y
- 1 cup coconut water
- Ice cubes optional
- 1/2 avocado, peeled and pitted
- 1/2 cup pineapple chunks
- 1/2 cup spinach leaves

Directions:

1. Combine avocado, pineapple pieces, spinach leaves, hemp seeds, and h2y in the blender.
2. Pour in coconut water for a tropical touch.
3. Blend till smooth, adding ice cubes for an added cold.
4. Pour into a glass and experience the creamy and nutrient-rich Avocado Bliss Booster!

Cinnamon Apple Pie Delight

Ingredients:

- 1 tbsp almond butter
- 1 tablespoon oats
- 1 cup unsweetened almond milk
- 1 apple, cored and cut
- 1/2 banana
- 1/2 teaspoon ground cinnamon
- Ice cubes optional

Directions:

1. Combine diced apple, banana, ground cinnamon, almond butter, oats, and almond milk in the blender.
2. Blend till smooth, adding ice cubes for an added cold.
3. Pour into a glass and experience the warm taste of Cinnamon Apple Pie Delight!

Tropical Green Tea Infusion

Ingredients:

- 1 tbsp chia seeds
- 1 tablespoon h2y
- Ice cubes optional
- 1/2 cup pineapple chunks
- 1/2 cup mango chunks
- 1 cup spinach leaves
- 1 green tea bag, steeped and cooled

Directions:

1. Combine pineapple pieces, mango chunks, spinach leaves, brewed green tea, chia seeds, and h2y in the blender.
2. Blend till smooth, adding ice cubes for a refreshing twist.

3. Pour into a glass and enjoy the Tropical Green Tea Infusion, a moisturizing and antioxidant-rich pleasure!

Healthy Biscotti Pumpkin

Ingredients:

- 3 eggs
- 2 tsp vanilla essence
- 3-thirds cup of general-purpose flour
- 1/4 teaspoon spice for pumpkin pie
- 1/4 tsp cinnamon
- ½ cup shredded dried apricots
- ¾ cup of pecans shredded
- 3 tablespoons of softened unsalted butter
- ½ cup pureed pumpkin
- 3 tablespoons of cream cheese without fat
- Brown sugar, 2 cup
- A smidgeon of baking powder
- 2-half tsp baking soda

- Salt, ¼ teaspoon
- 2 egg
- 2 tablespoon of water

Directions:
1. Be aware that the dish must be refrigerated for 3 hours before baking!
2. Finely shred the pecans and apricots individually using a food processor or by hand. Put away.
3. Using an electric mixer, beat butter in a large bowl at medium to high speed for 30 seconds. Add sugar, baking soda, baking powder, cinnamon, pumpkin spice, fat-free cream cheese, and salt, and beat until well blended. Add pumpkin puree and beat.
4. Mix the 3 eggs and vanilla until well blended. Using the mixer, beat in as much of the flour as possible. Using a big spoon, stir in any leftover flour.

5. Add the apricots and pecans and stir until well combined. For 3 hours, or until the dough is manageable, cover and chill.
6. 350°F, or 175 degrees Celsius, should be the oven temperature. Next, coat a large cookie sheet with nonstick cooking spray or cover it with parchment paper. Split the dough in 3. Each half of the biscotti dough should be shaped into a 12-inch long log that is ½-3/4 inch high and 4 inches broad. On a baking sheet that has been prepped or lined with parchment, space the logs about 2 inches apart.
7. To prepare an egg wash, beat together 2 egg and 2 tablespoon of water. Drizzle the egg mixture onto the loaves.
8. Bake loaves for 25 to 30 minutes, or until they are light brown, in a preheated oven.
9. Place the loaves on the cookie sheet and allow them to cool fully for about 1 hour.

Handmade Potato Cakes

Ingredients:

- 3 tsp finely grated Parmesan cheese
- A pinch of pepper and salt
- 2-teaspoon cajun spice
- 2 tsp of salt with garlic
- 1/4 tsp paprika
- 4 medley potatoes
- 3 eggs
- 3 tsp of flour
- 4 cooked and crumbled centre-cut bacon pieces; save the bacon fat in the pan

Directions:

1. After slicing and peeling the potatoes, boil them for about eight minutes. Allow to cool.

In case you are pressed for time, give them a quick wash with cold water.
2. Mash the potatoes in a big basin using a cheese grater.
3. Add the cooked bacon, eggs, flour, parmesan, and spices, and stir well.
4. Make ten patties, each using about ¼ cup of the potato mixture.
5. Reheat the bacon oil that was left behind after the bacon was cooked. Fry patties, rotating them from time to time, for at least five minutes on each side. To remove extra fat, drain the potato cakes onto a paper towel and serve warm. Have fun!

Steel-Cut Oats With Lemon Blueberries

Ingredients:

- 3 tsp of sugar
- 2 tsp of lemon zest
- 1/4 tsp salt
- 1 cup blueberries, either frozen or fresh
- Half a cup of chia seeds
- 2 tablespoon of butter.
- Oats, 2 cup, steel-cut
- 4 cups of water
- 1/2 cup of condensed milk

Directions:

1. In the pressure cooker, add the butter and choose Sauté. After melting the butter, add the oats and toast for approximately 4

minutes, turning often, until they start to smell nutty.
2. Stir in the salt, sugar, zest, water, and half-and-half. Choose high pressure and give the cooking duration 10 minutes.
3. The pressure cooker should be turned off when the buzzer sounds. After using a natural pressure release for ten minutes, quickly release any residual pressure. Remove the cover gently once the valve lowers.
4. Toss oats. Add chia seeds and blueberries and stir. After the oats reach the proper thickness, cover them and let them rest for five minutes.
5. Add more blueberries, agave or h2y, sliced almonds, and a dash of milk over top.

Hazelnut And Pumpkin Flaugnarde Clafoutis

Ingredients:

- 1 cup milk 1%.
- 2 teaspoon of vanilla extract
- Split 2-inch vanilla bean with pulp removed
- 8 tsp of cinnamon
- 1/8 tsp. nuts
- 8 tsp of ginger
- 1/3 cup canned or homemade pureed pumpkin
- Frying oil
- 4 big eggs
- 3 big egg whites
- 10 tablespoons sugar or mild agave nectar
- Sift 1/2 cup of unbleached general-purpose flour

- A little salt

- Hazelnuts, 1/3 cup, diced, gently roasted

Directions:

1. Turn the oven on to 425°F. Grease a nine-inch pie dish with cooking spray.
2. Sprinkle the dish with the hazelnuts.
3. In a blender or food processor, combine the eggs, egg whites, agave, milk, vanilla bean, extract, cinnamon, nutmeg, ginger, and salt. Process in blender until smooth, about 30 seconds.
4. Blend in the pumpkin purée after adding it.
5. Pulse in the flour until well-mixed.
6. Fill the pie plate with the batter.
7. Bake at 375°F for 12 minutes, or until the centre is just set, after 15 minutes of baking.
8. Serve right away.

Smoothie With Tropical Green Blast

Ingredients:

- 1/3 of a cup of pineapple chunks
- ¼ cup of orange juice
- 2 cups fresh spinach leaves 1 banana, diced
- 1/3 cup ripe mango dice

Directions:

1. In the blender, combine spinach, banana, mango, pineapple, and orange juice in this sequence. Mix until all Ingredients: are combined this will take about 90 minutes on high speed.
2. Add the milk and blend until completely combined and creamy.
3. Pour into a glass and enjoy.

Smoothie Caramel Banana Green

Ingredients:

- 1 teaspoon of caramel store-bought
- 1 teaspoon walnuts
- ½ cup canned coconut milk
- 1 cup chopped spinach
- 1 cup sliced bananas
- ½ cup nonfat milk soya, oat, almond, hemp or rice

Directions:

1. Combine spinach, coconut, and non-dairy milk in a blender. Mix until well combined.
2. Stir in the bananas, caramel, and walnuts. Mix until completely smooth.
3. Transfer to a large glass and serve.

Mango Spinach Green Smoothie

Ingredients:

- 2 tbsp. desiccated coconut
- 2 tbsp dried raisins
- ½ cup of oat milk can be substituted with any non-dairy milk
- ½ cup of water
- 1 cup fresh spinach leaves
- ½ cup ripe fresh mango chunks
- ½ tablespoon linseeds

Directions:
1. Combine spinach, oat milk, and water in a mixing bowl.
2. Add mangoes, linseeds, desiccated coconut, and raisins and blend on high until smooth.
3. Transfer to a large glass and serve.

Spinach And Feta Omelet With Whole Grain Toast

Ingredients:

- 1/4 cup crumbled feta cheese
- Salt and pepper to taste
- 1 teaspn olive oil
- 2 large eggs
- 1 cup fresh spinach, chopped
- 1 slice whole grain bread

Directions:

1. Beat the eggs in a bowl until they are thoroughly mixed. Add salt and pepper to season.
2. In a nonstick skillet over medium heat, warm the olive oil.
3. Stir in the chopped spinach and cook for 2-3 minutes, or until wilted.

4. Cover the spinach in the skillet with the beaten eggs.
5. Give the eggs a minute to boil quietly so that the edges begin to firm.
6. Use a spatula to gently lift the omelet's borders and tilt the skillet so that the uncooked eggs can flow to the outside.
7. Distribute the feta cheese crumbles equally over the omelet.
8. Cook the eggs for a further 2 to 3 minutes, or until they are fully set and the cheese has melted.
9. Using the spatula, gently fold the omelet in half and transfer it to a plate.
10. Toast the whole-grain bread slice until it is crisp and brown.
11. Place the whole grain toast on the side and serve the spinach and feta omelet.

Capers Salad With Fresh Mozzarella, Tomatoes, Basil Leaves, And Balsamic Glaze

Ingredients:

- 1 large tomato or 2
- 2 tbspns balsamic glaze medium-sized tomatoes
- Salt and pepper to taste
- 8 ounces fresh mozzarella
- Cheese
- A handful of fresh basil leaves
- Extra-virgin olive oil for drizzling optional

Directions:

1. Cut the fresh mozzarella cheese and tomatoes into roughly 1/4-inch-thick slices.
2. Position the tomato slices on a tray or serving plate.

3. Top each piece of tomato with a fresh mozzarella slice.
4. Place a fresh basil leaf over each slice of mozzarella.
5. Continue layering until the tomato, mozzarella, and basil areall used.
6. Glaze the tomato, basil, mozzarella, and balsamic vinegar with balsamic vinegar.
7. To taste, add salt and pepper to the dish.
8. Add extra virgin olive oil to the salad if desired.
9. Immediately serve the Capers salad.

Grilled Lamb Chops With Roasted Sweet Potatoes And Greek Salad

Ingredients:

- 2 cups mixed salad greens
- 1/2 cucumber, diced
- 1/2 red onion, thinly sliced
- 1 cup cherry tomatoes, halved
- 1/4 cup Kalamata olives
- 1/4 cup crumbled feta cheese
- 1 lemon of juice
- 2 tbspns extra-virgin olive oil
- 4 lamb chops
- Salt and pepper to taste
- 2 tbspns olive oil

- 2 medium sweet potatoes, peeled and cut into cubes
- 1 teaspn dried oregano
- 1 teaspn paprika
- 1/2 teaspn garlic powder
- 1/2 teaspn onion powder
- Salt and pepper to taste

Directions:
1. Turn the grill's heat up to medium-high. Add salt and pepper to both sides of the lamb chops. Drizzle olive oil over the lamb chops and rub to evenly coat.
2. Combine the onion powder, garlic powder, paprika, and dried oregano in a mixing dish.
3. Use a light touch to gently press the spice mixture onto the lamb chops.
4. 5 minutes per side for medium-rare, until you achieve your d2ness desire.

5. Set the oven to 400°F 200°C while the lamb chops are roasting.
6. Combine the olive oil, salt, and pepper with the sweet potato cubes in a different baking dish.
7. Roast the sweet potatoes for 20 to 25 minutes in a preheated oven until they are golden and soft, tossing once halfway through.
8. Combine the salad greens, sliced cherry tomatoes, Kalamata olives, diced cucumber, red onion, and feta cheese in a sizable mixing dish.
9. To make the dressing, combine the extra virgin olive oil, lemon juice, salt, and pepper in a small bowl.
10. After adding the dressing, mix the salad items to properly distribute the coating.
11. Place the roasted sweet potatoes, Greek salad, and grilled lamb chops on a serving plate. Serve right away.

Hummus With Whole Grain Crackers And Carrot Sticks

Ingredients:

- 2 tbspns lemon juice
- 2 cloves garlic, minced
- 2 tbspns extra-virgin olive oil
- 1 can 15 ounces chickpeas, drained and rinsed
- 1/4 cup tahini
- 1/2 teaspn ground cumin Salt and pepper to taste Whole grain crackers, for serving
- Carrot sticks, for serving

Directions:

1. Blend or process the drained and rinsed chickpeas with the tahini, lemon juice, garlic powder, olive oil, cumin, salt, and pepper.

2. Pulse the mixture a second time to make it smooth and creamy, scraping the sides as necessary.
3. To get the right consistency, add a little water or extra olive oil if the hummus is too thick.
4. Taste the hummus and, if necessary, add additional salt, pepper, or lemon juice to suit your tastes.
5. Pour the hummus into a serving dish.
6. Put carrot sticks and whole grain crackers on the side and serve the hummus with them.

7.

www.ingramcontent.com/pod-product-compliance
Lightning Source LLC
LaVergne TN
LVHW020437070526
838199LV00063B/4771